CRAZY

Coloring Book For Adults

AMAZINGLY RELAXING INSANITY

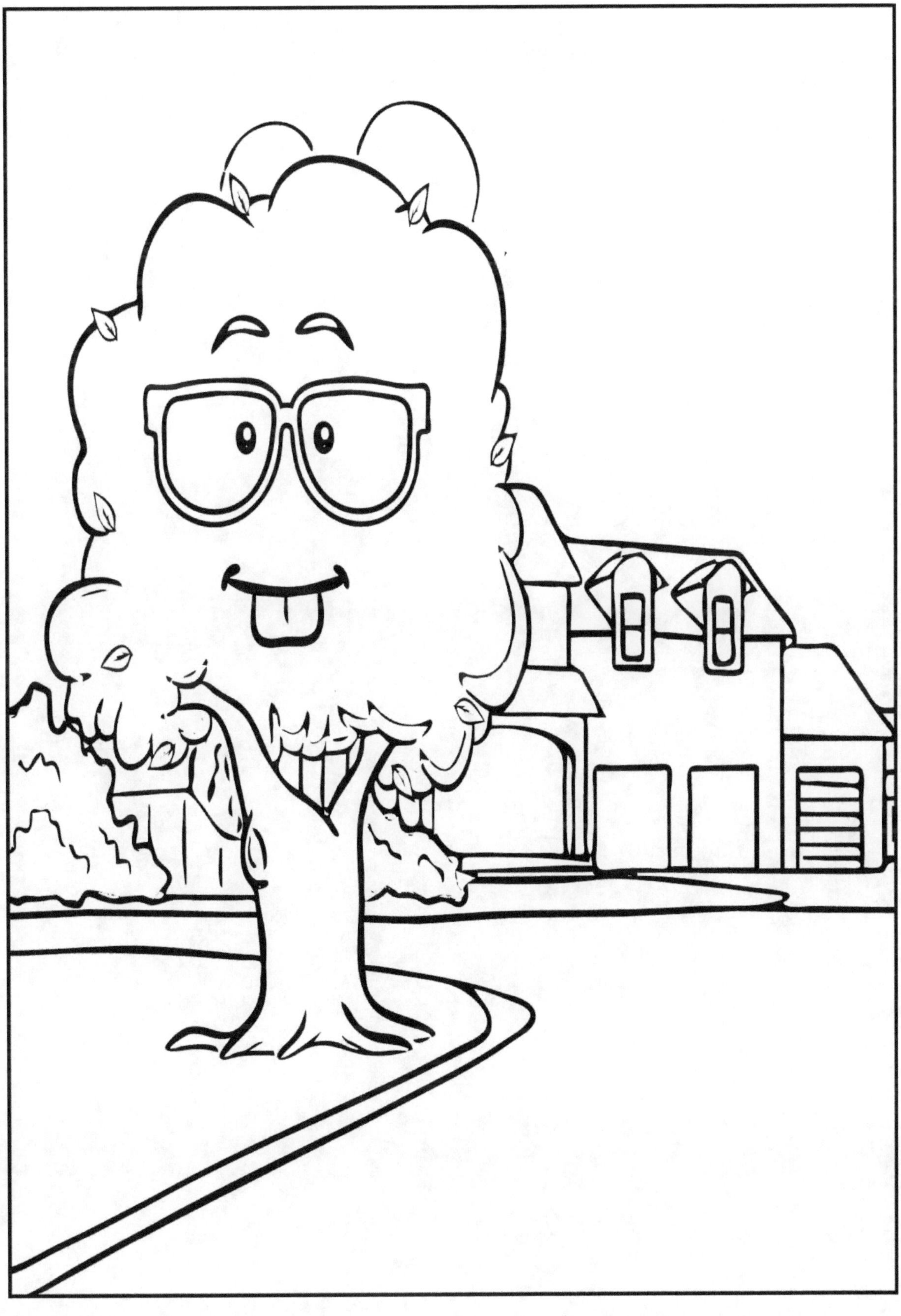

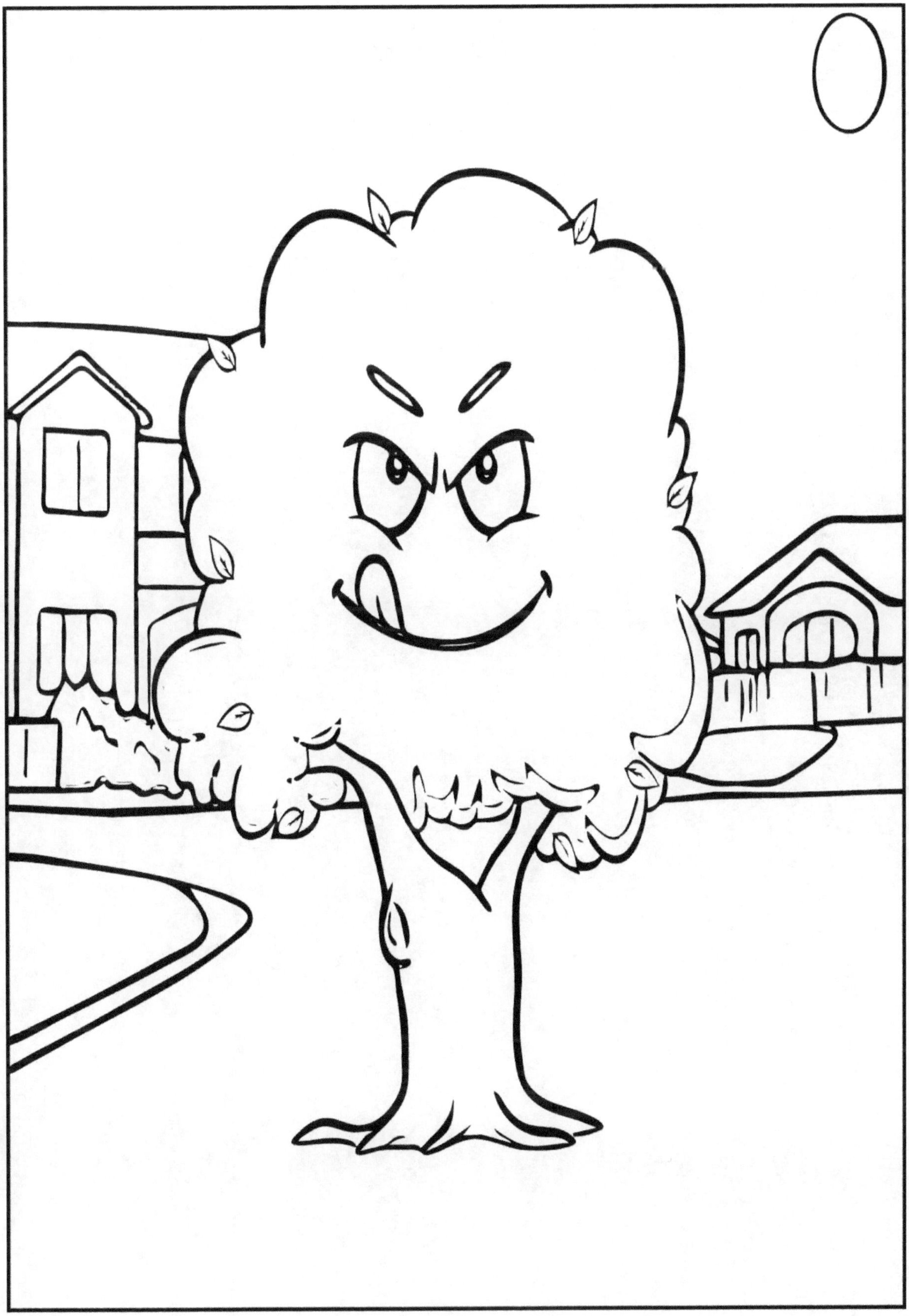

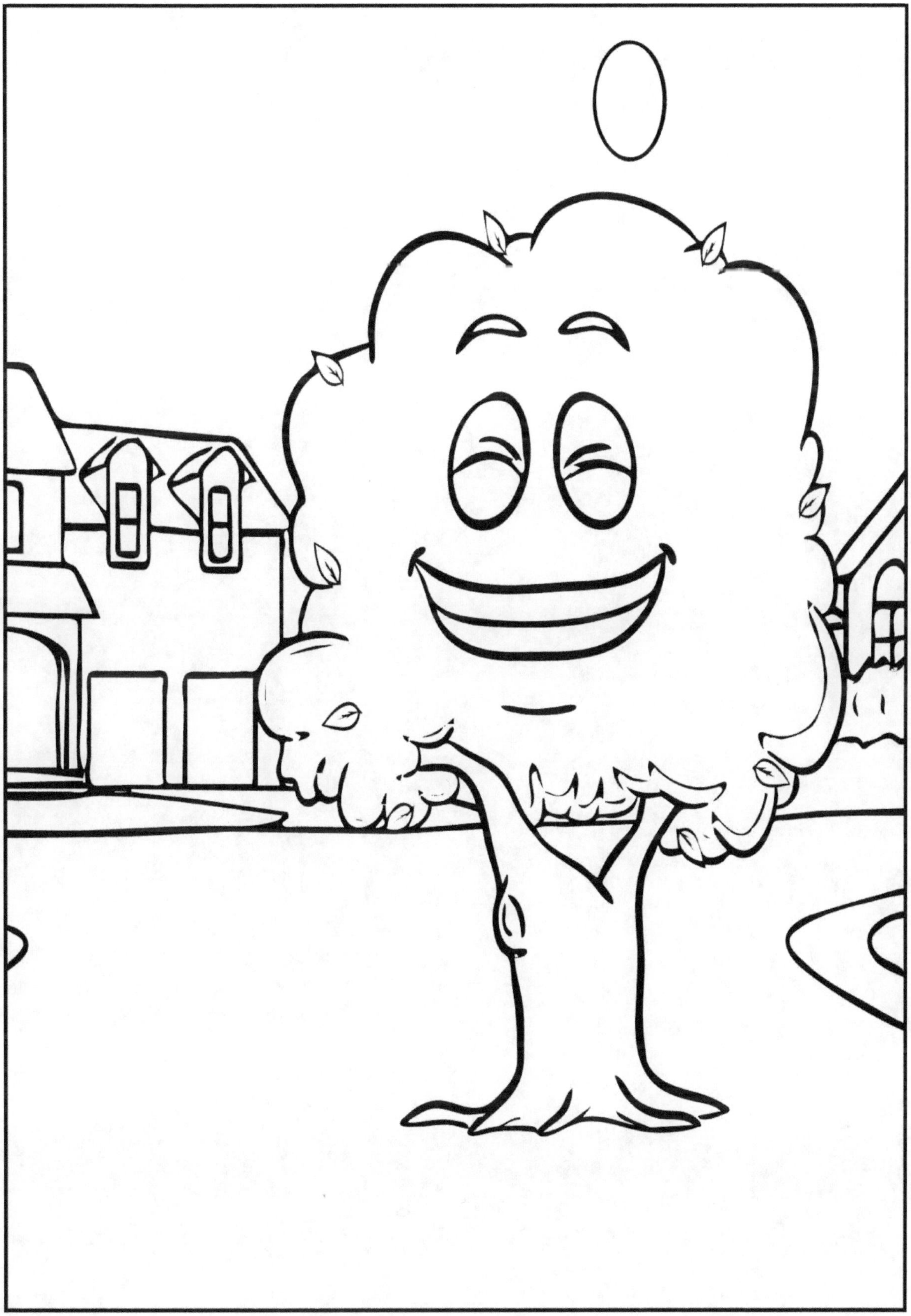

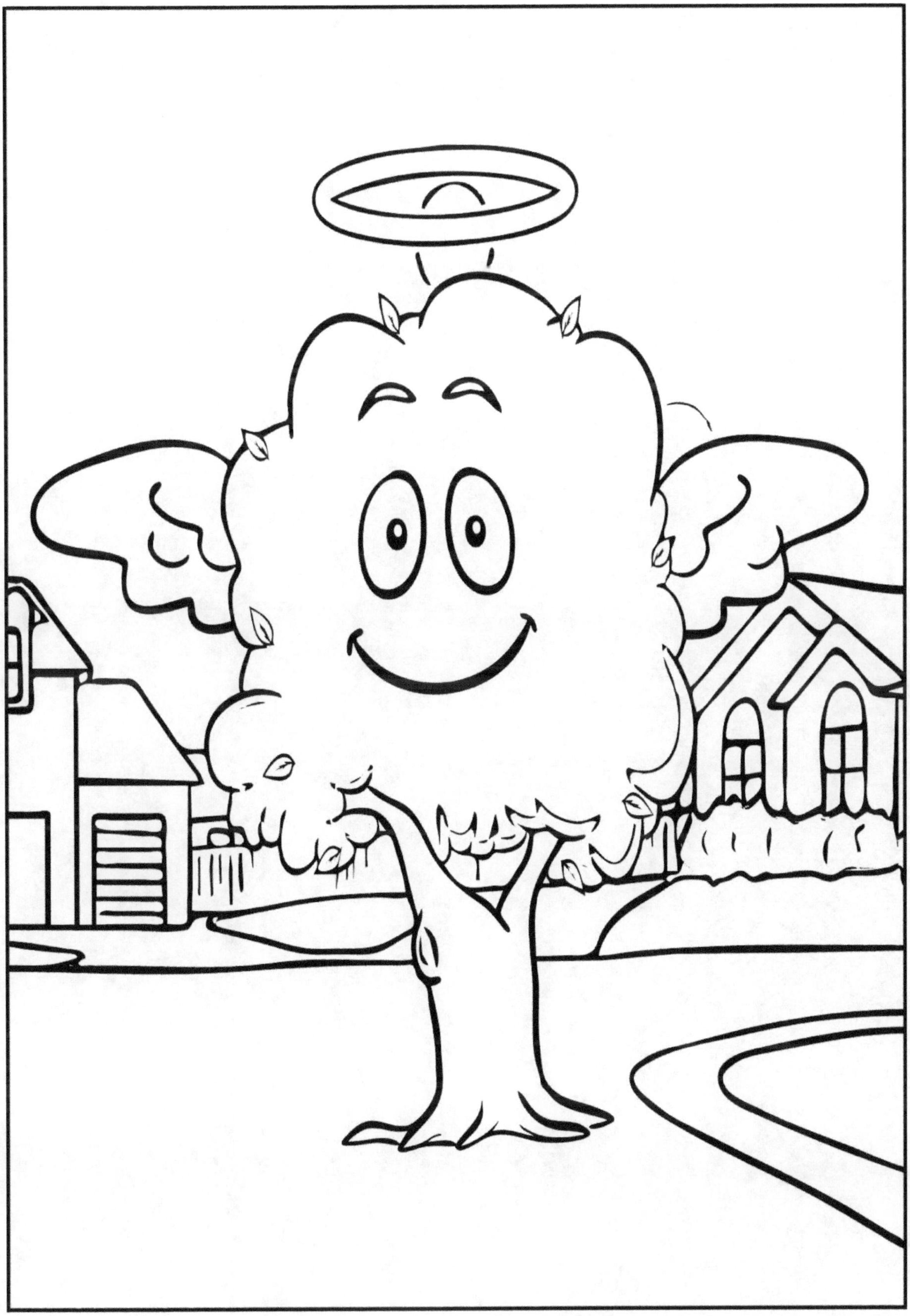

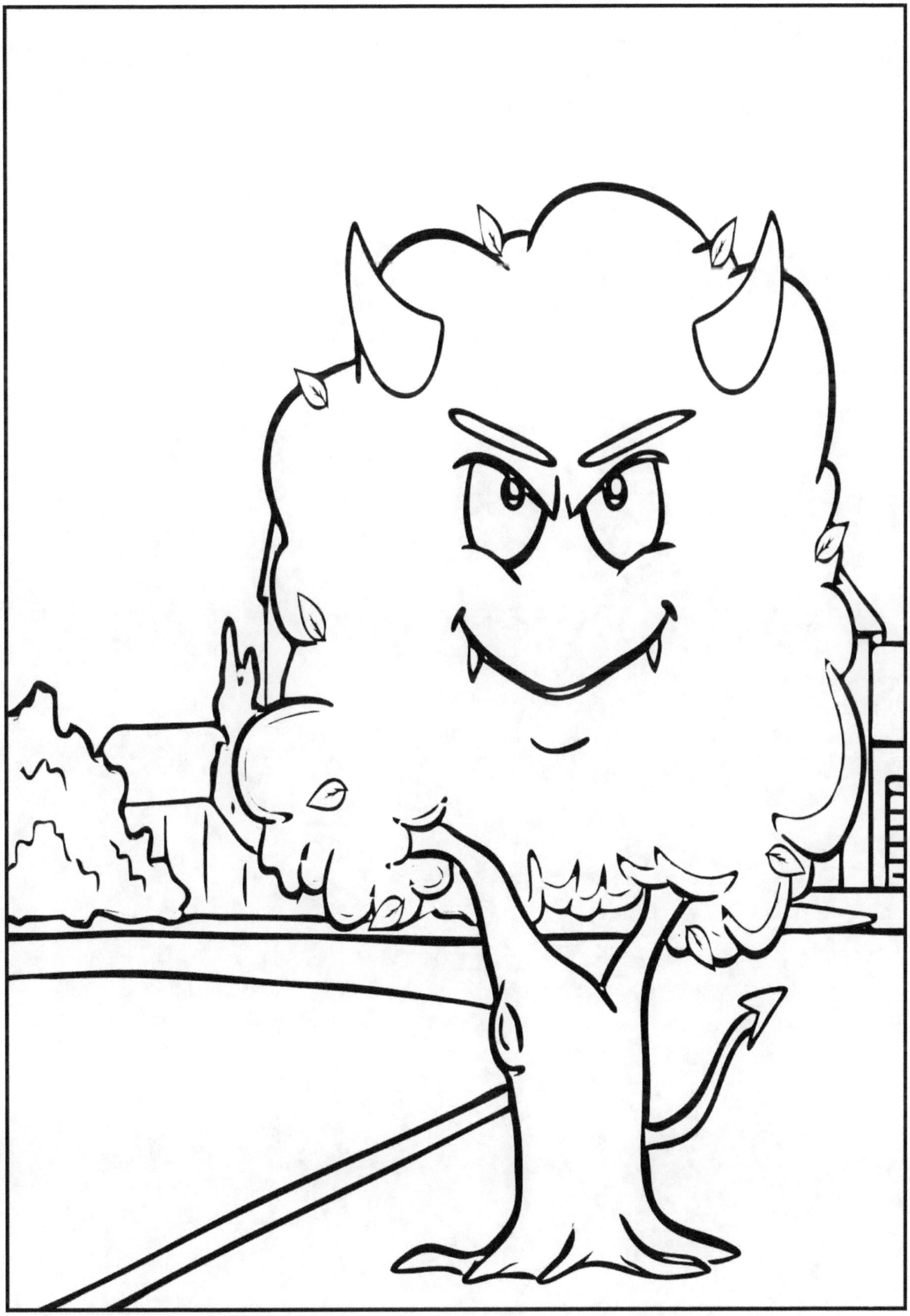

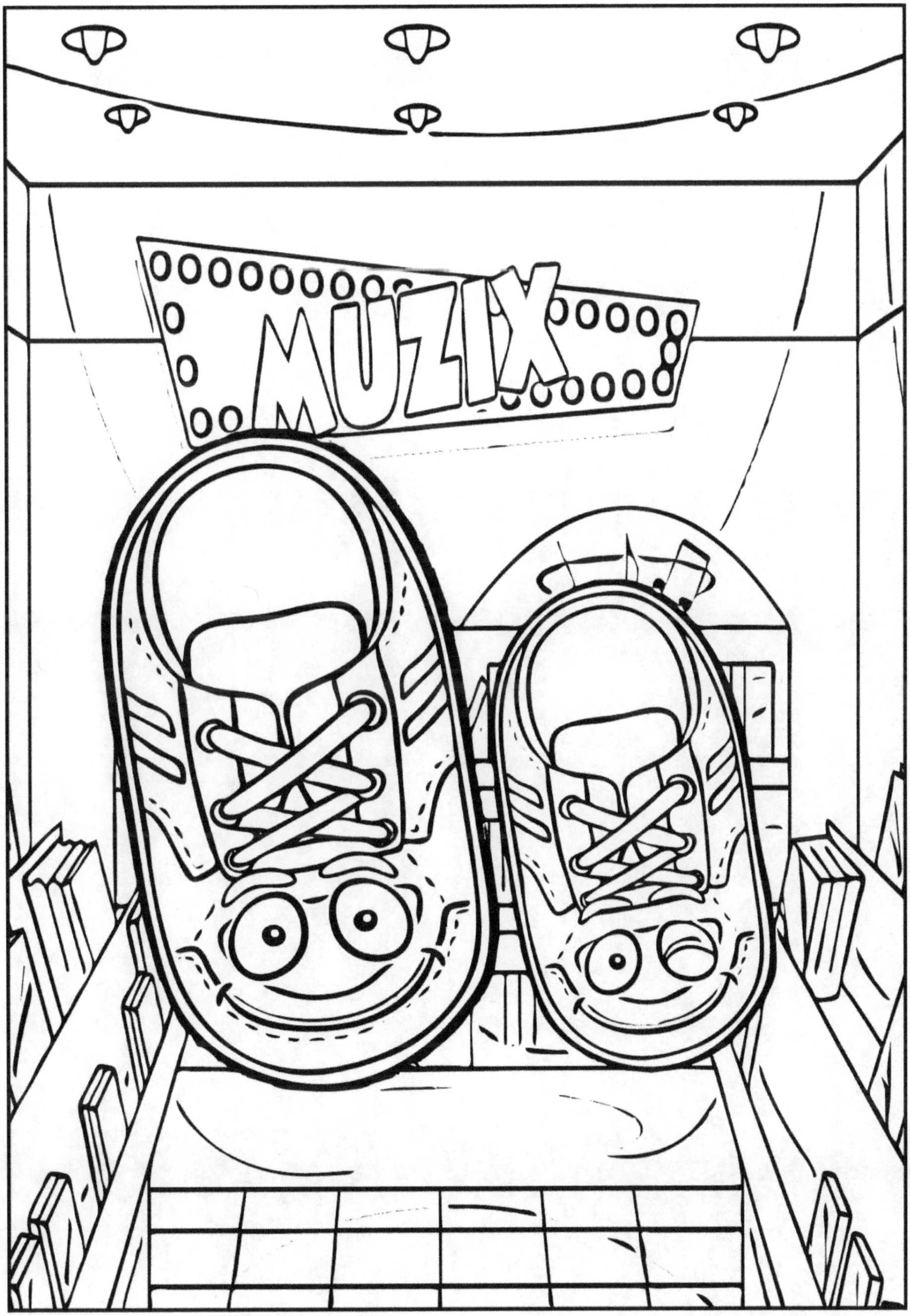
MUZIX

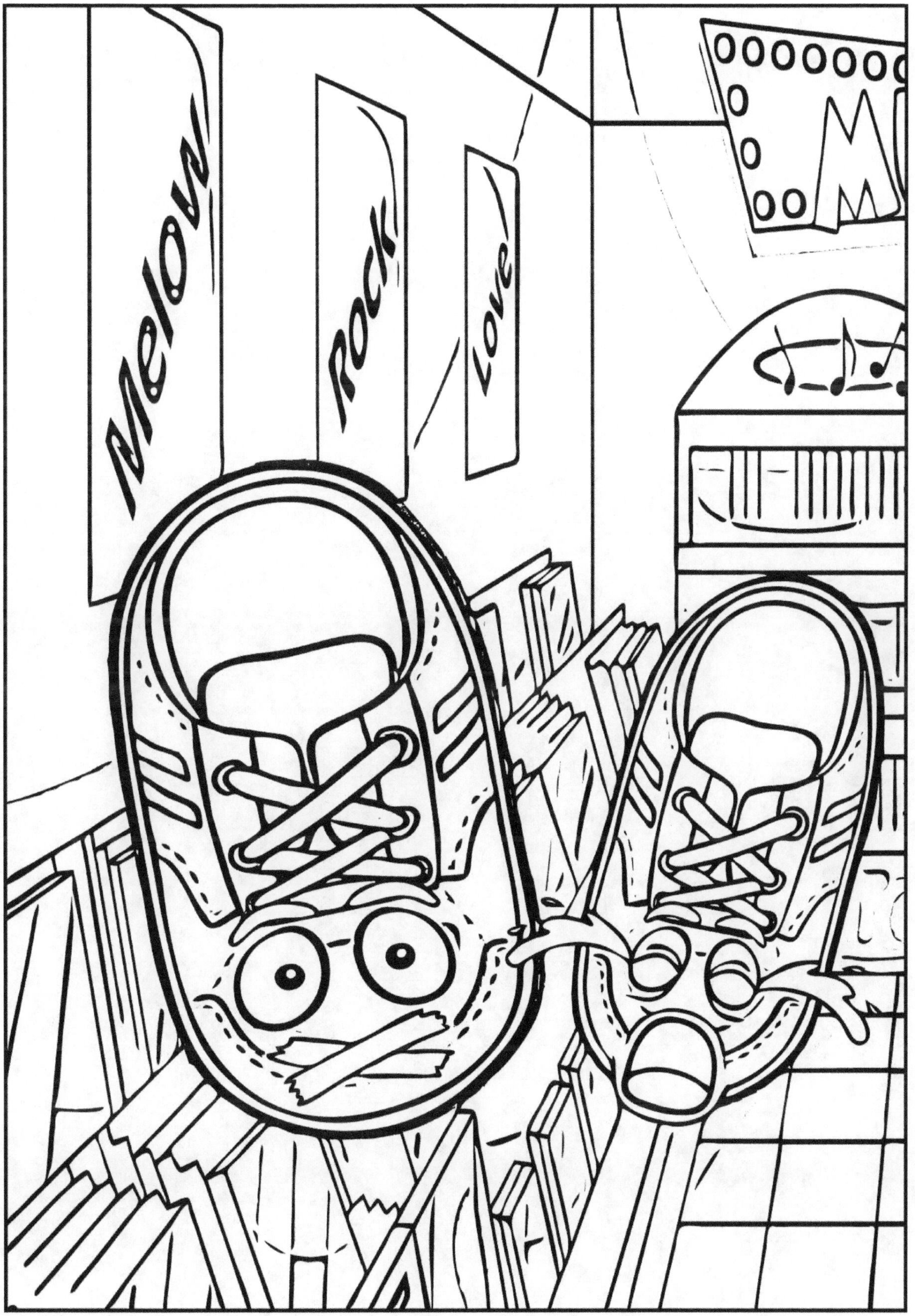
Mellow
Rock
Love

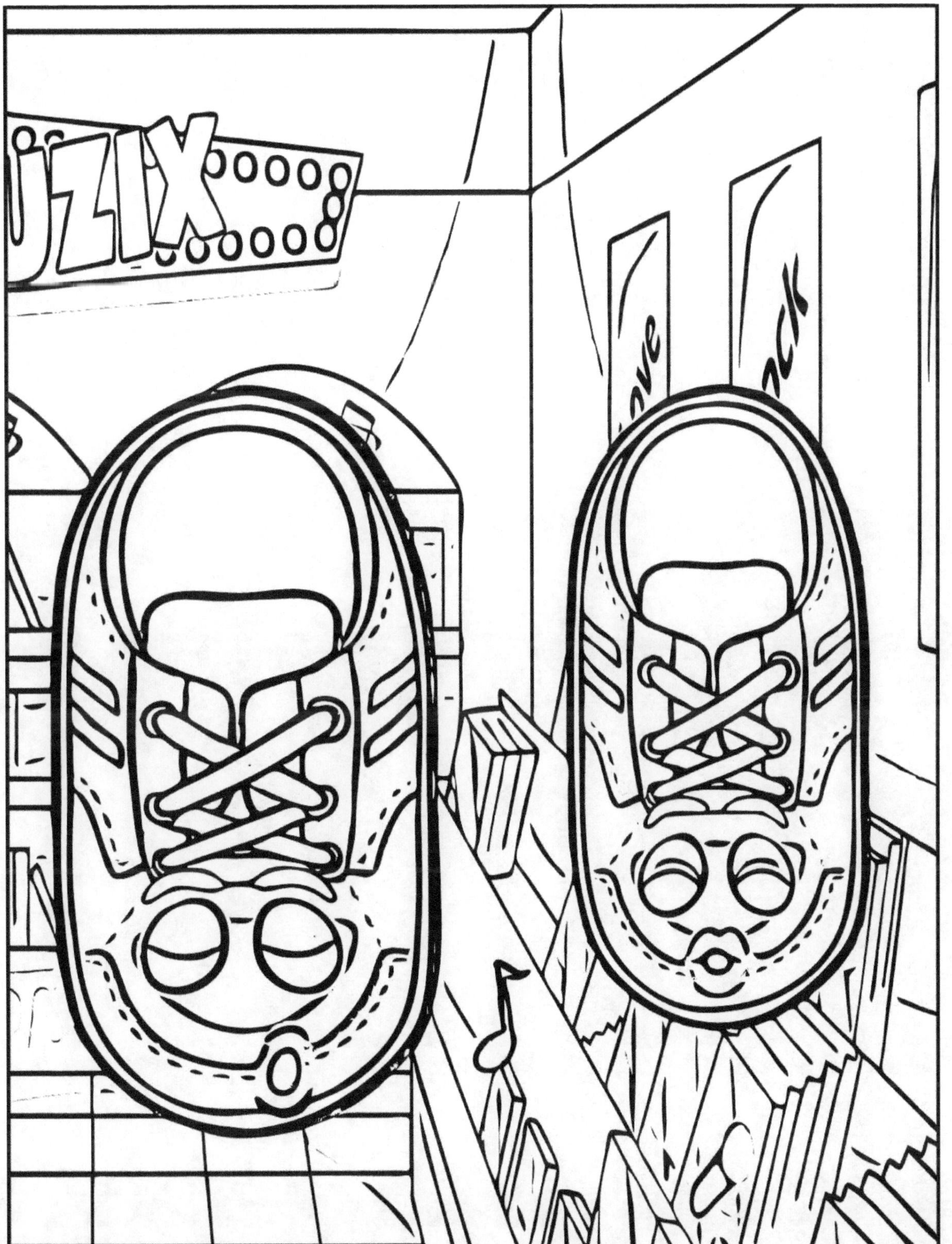

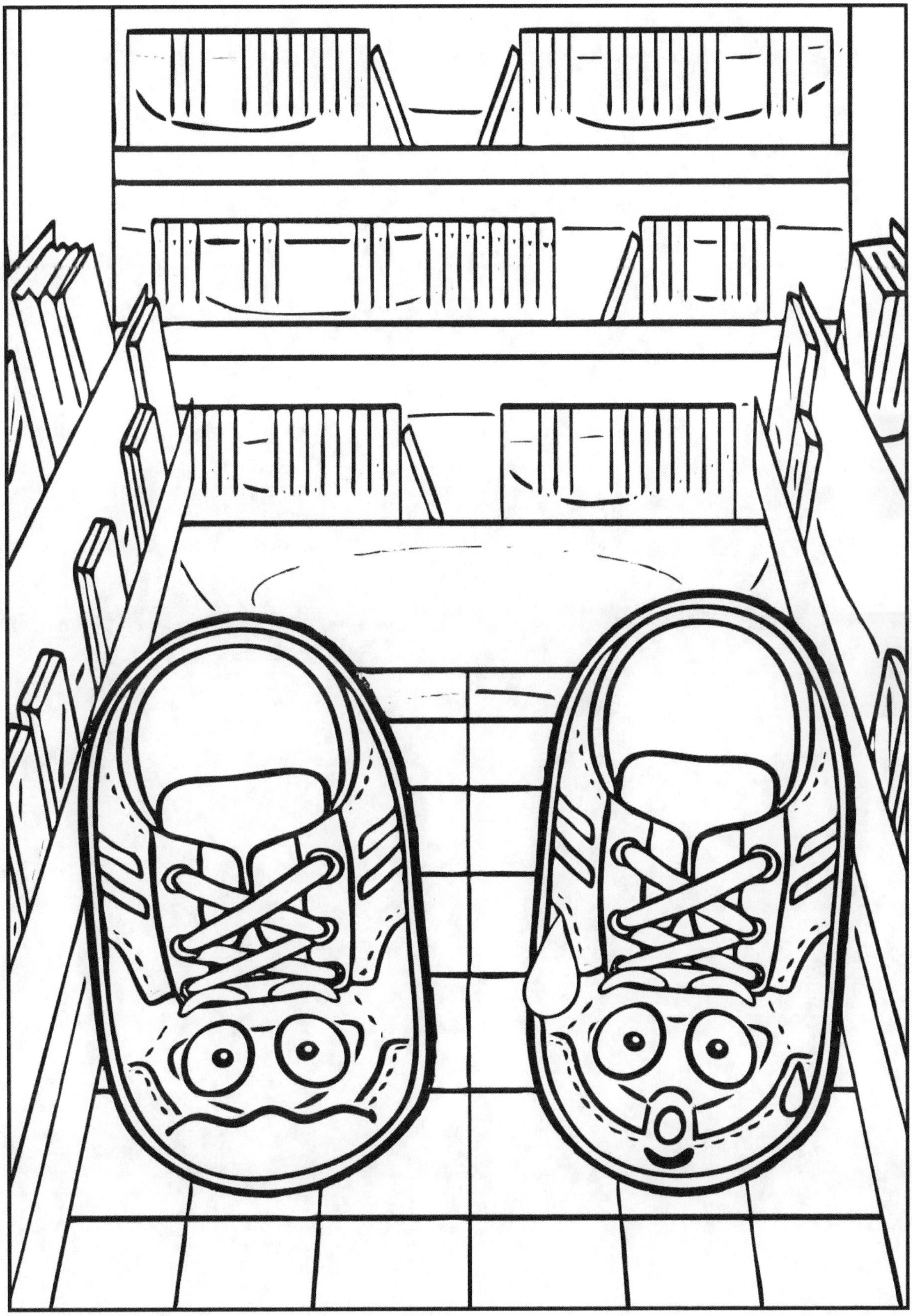

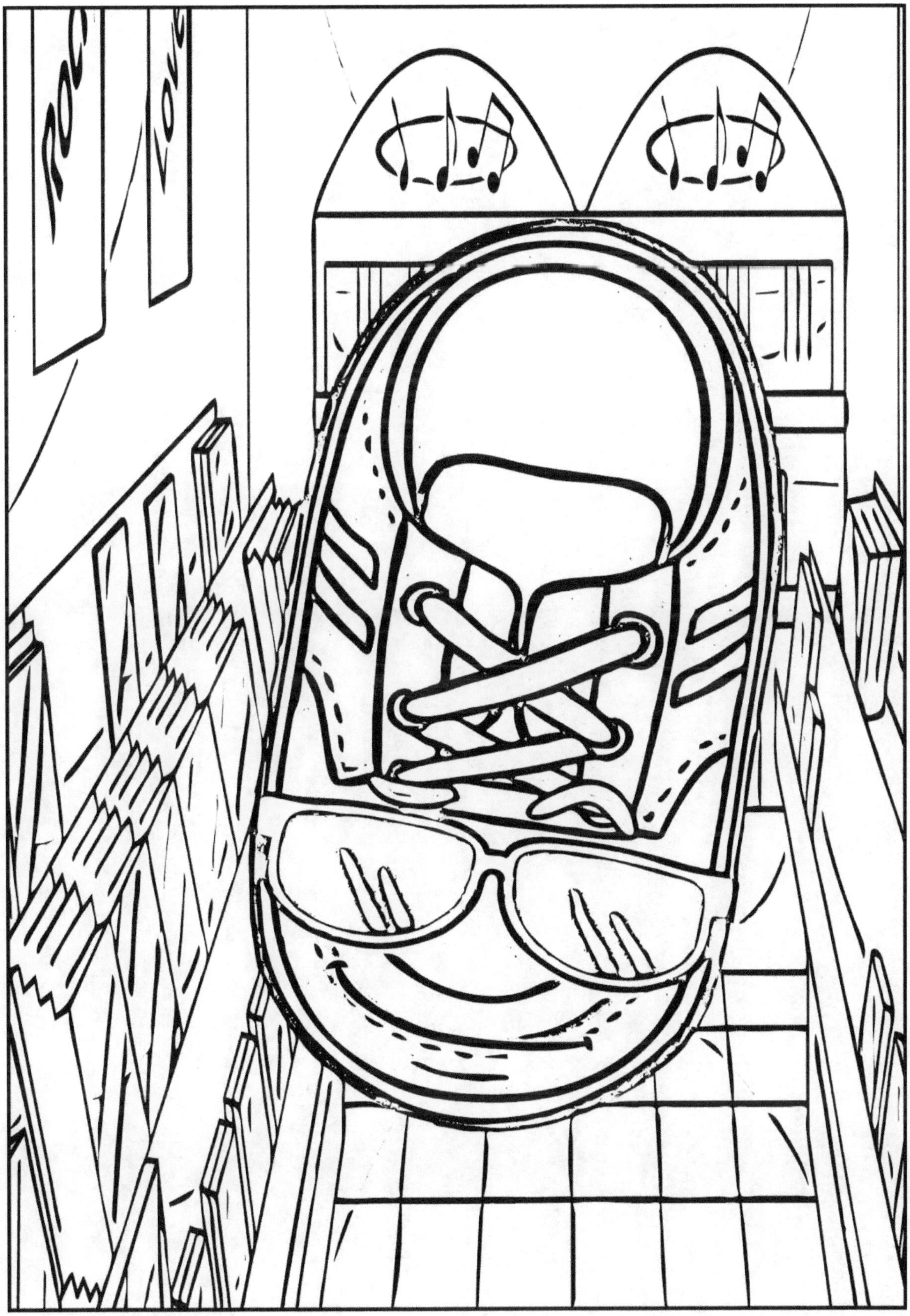

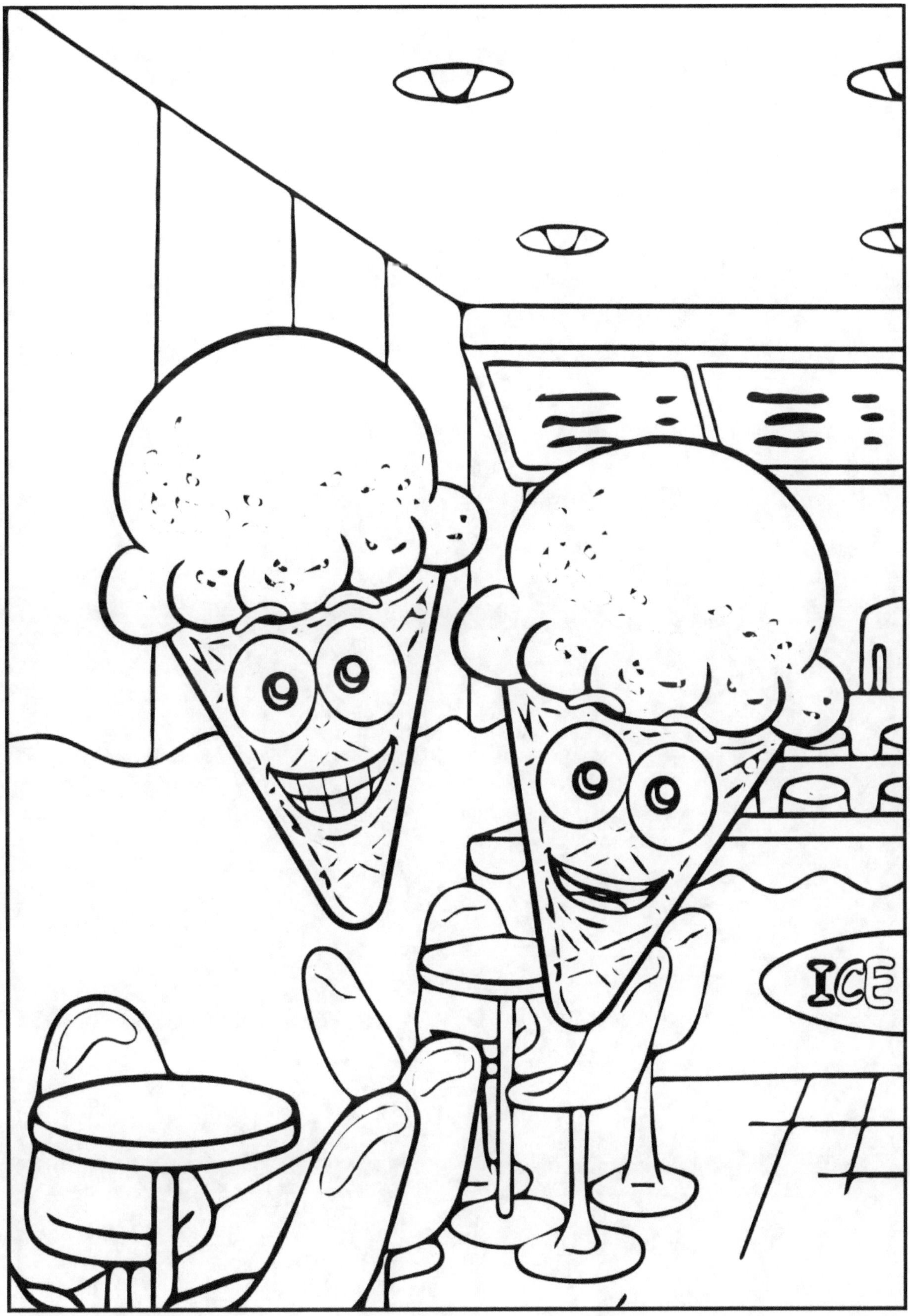
ICE

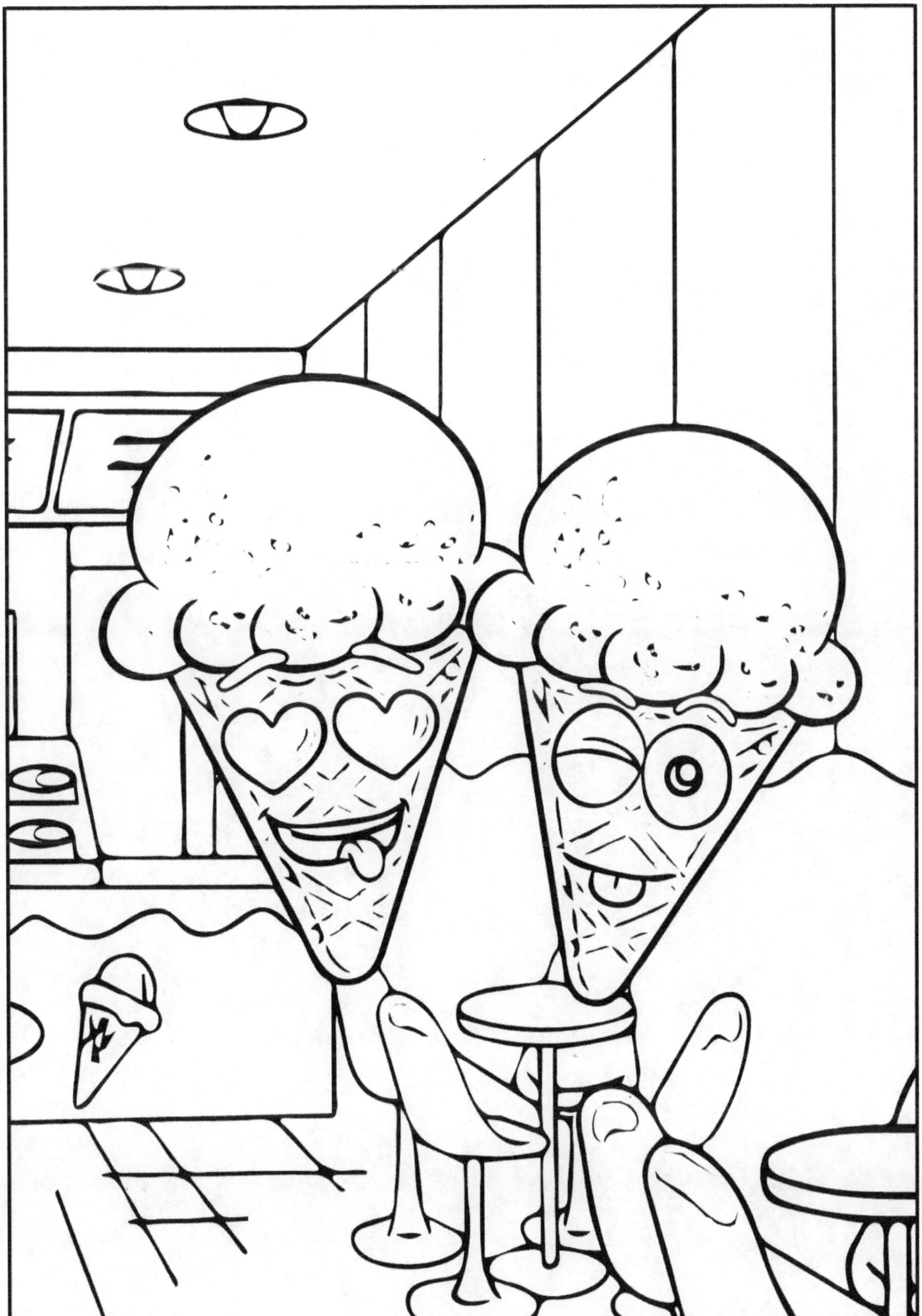

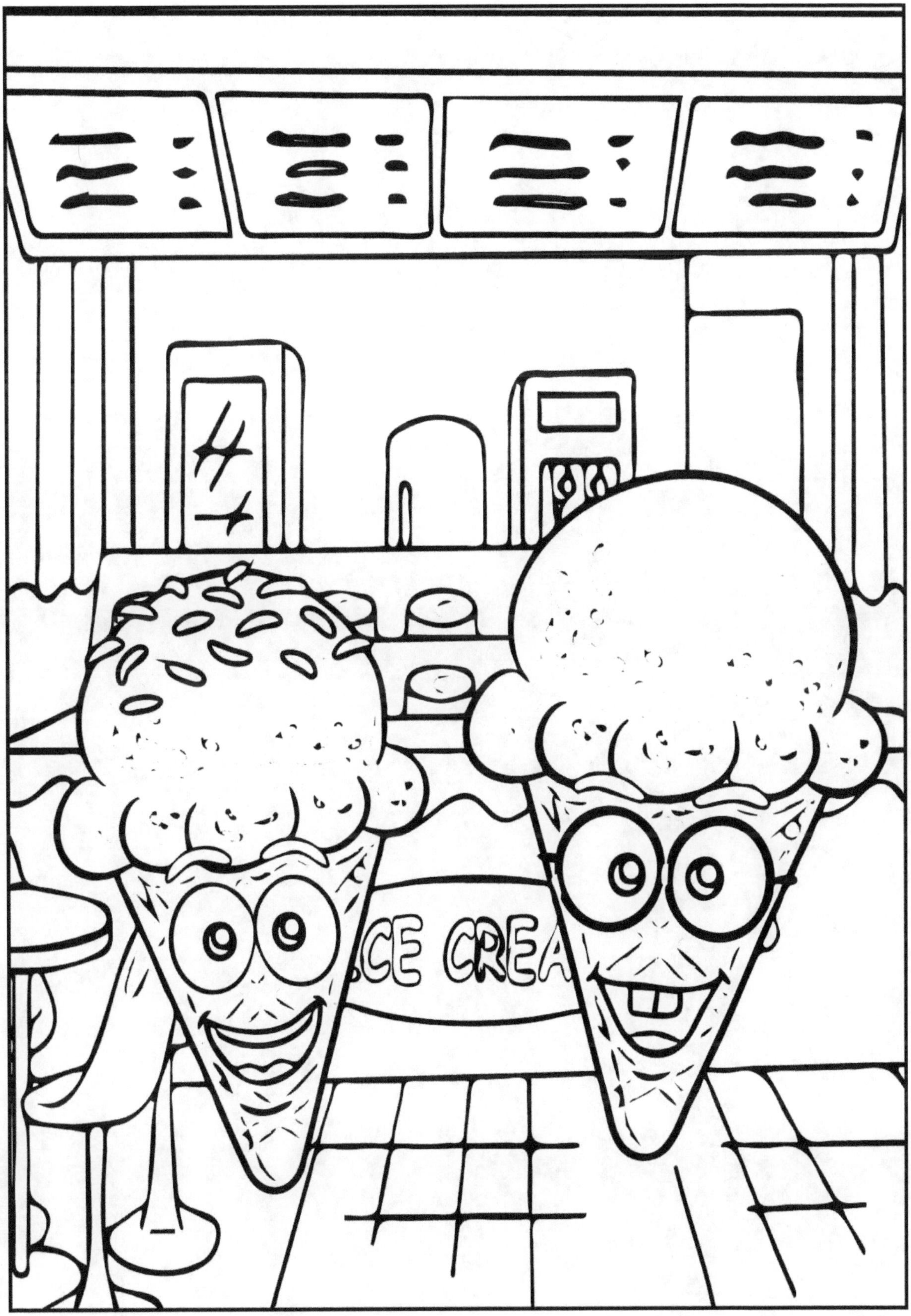
CE CREA

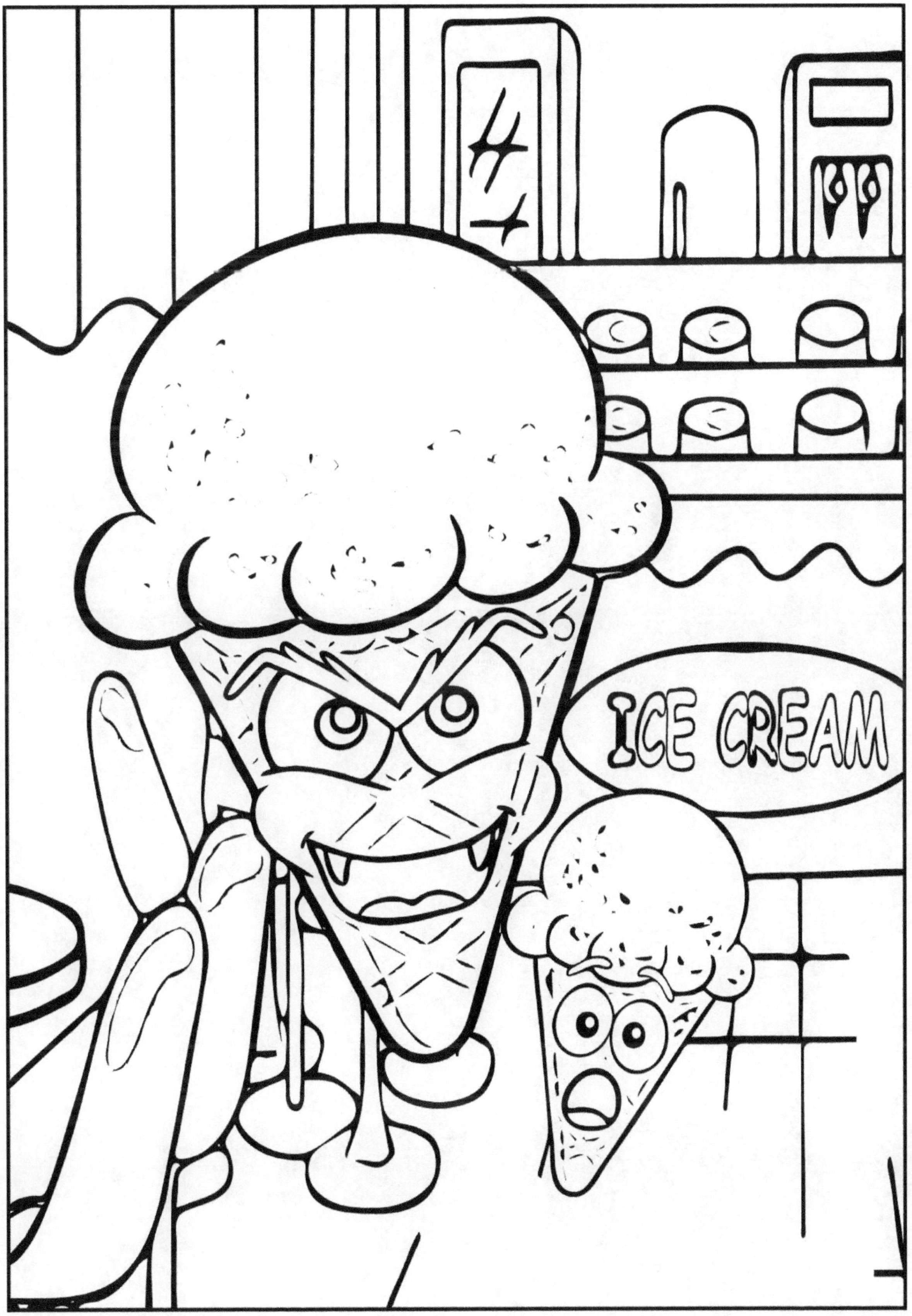
ICE CREAM

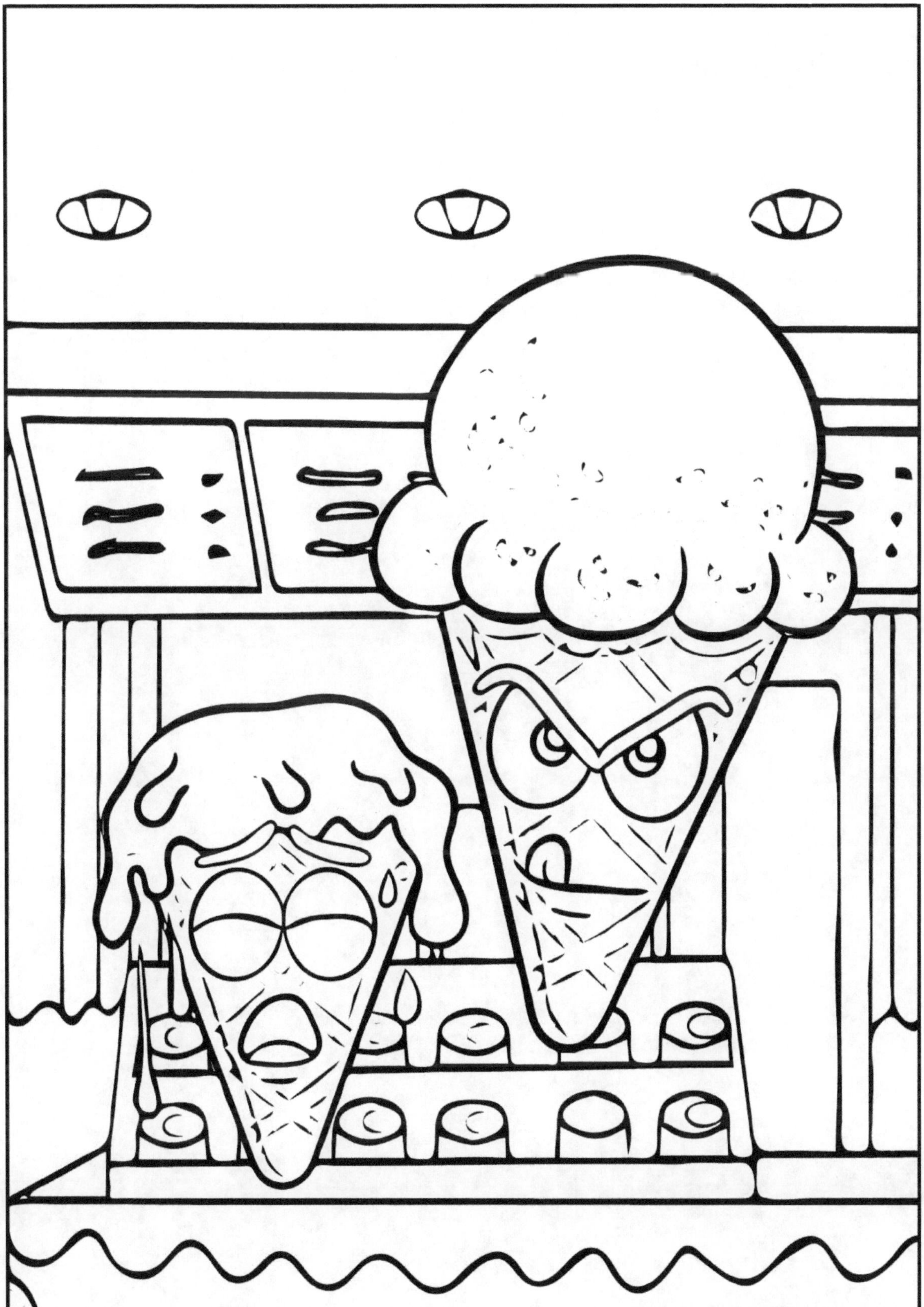

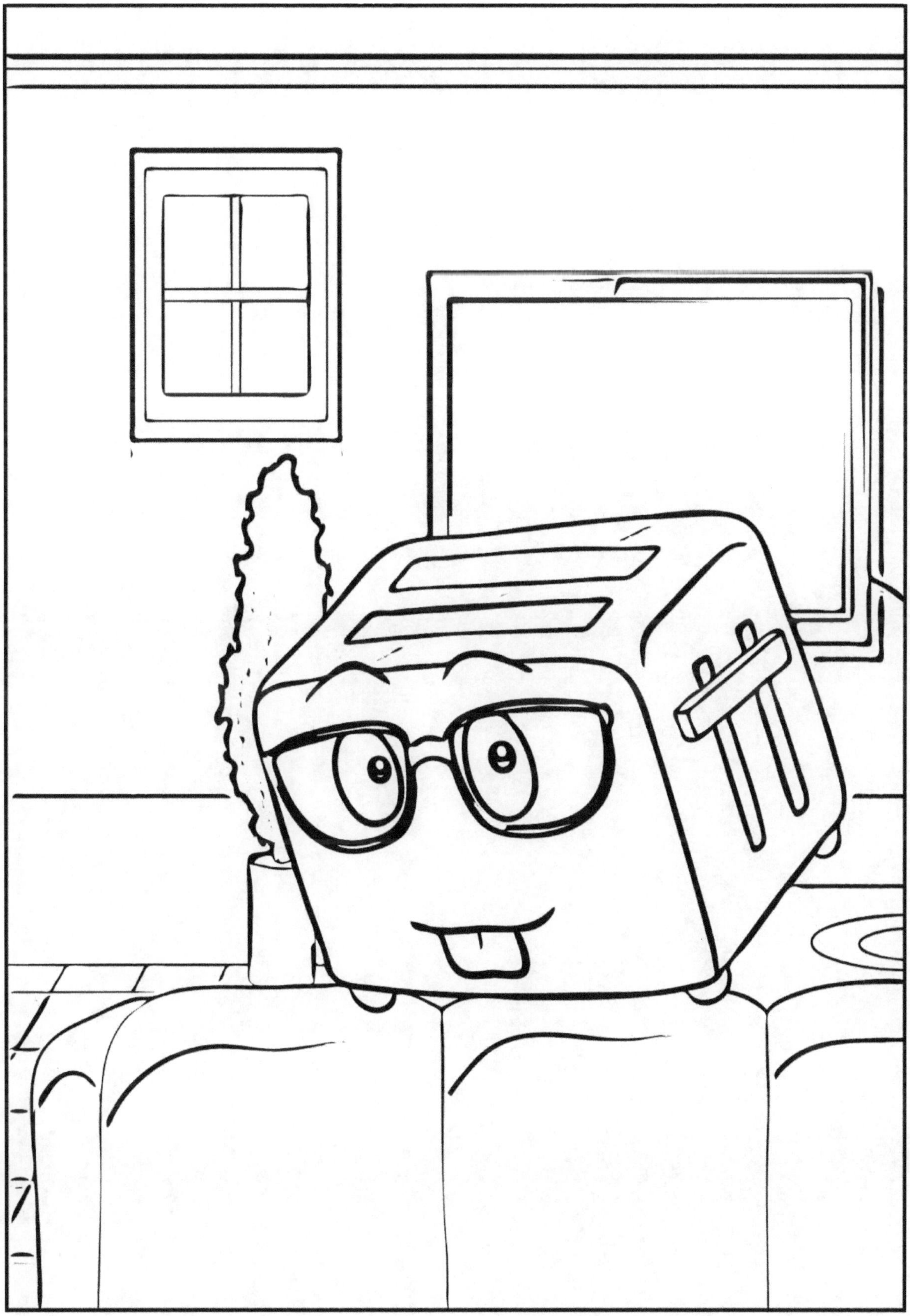

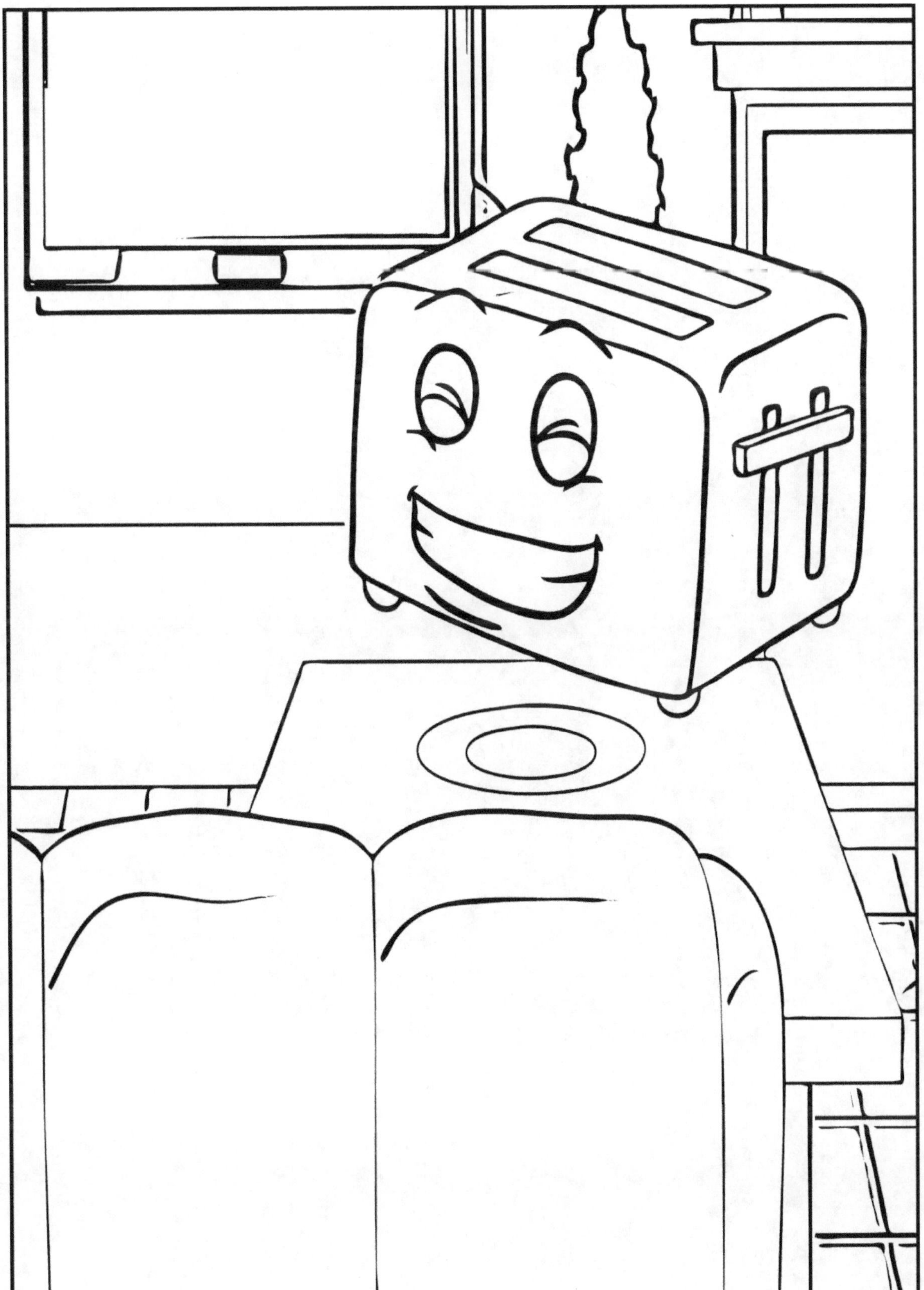

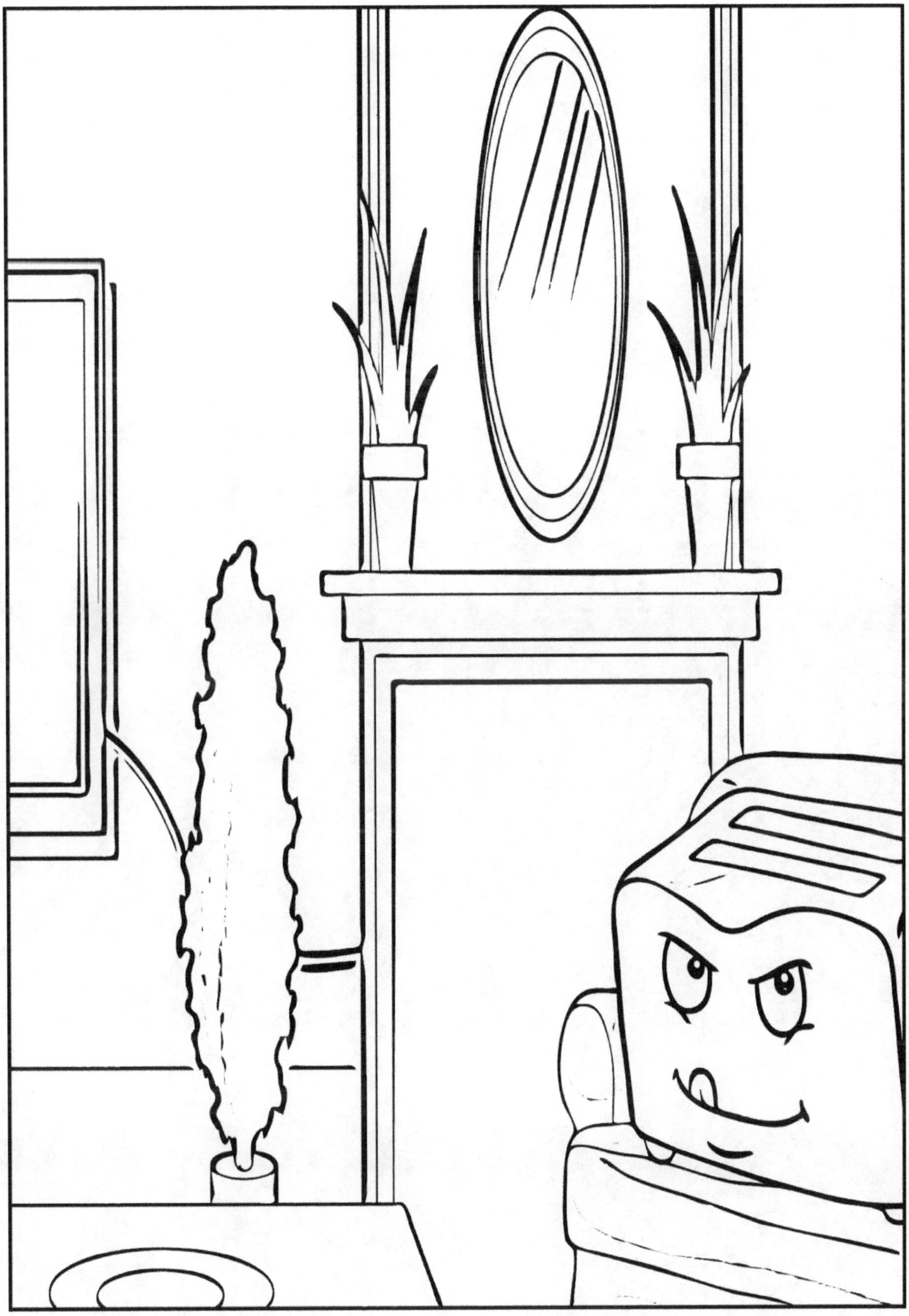

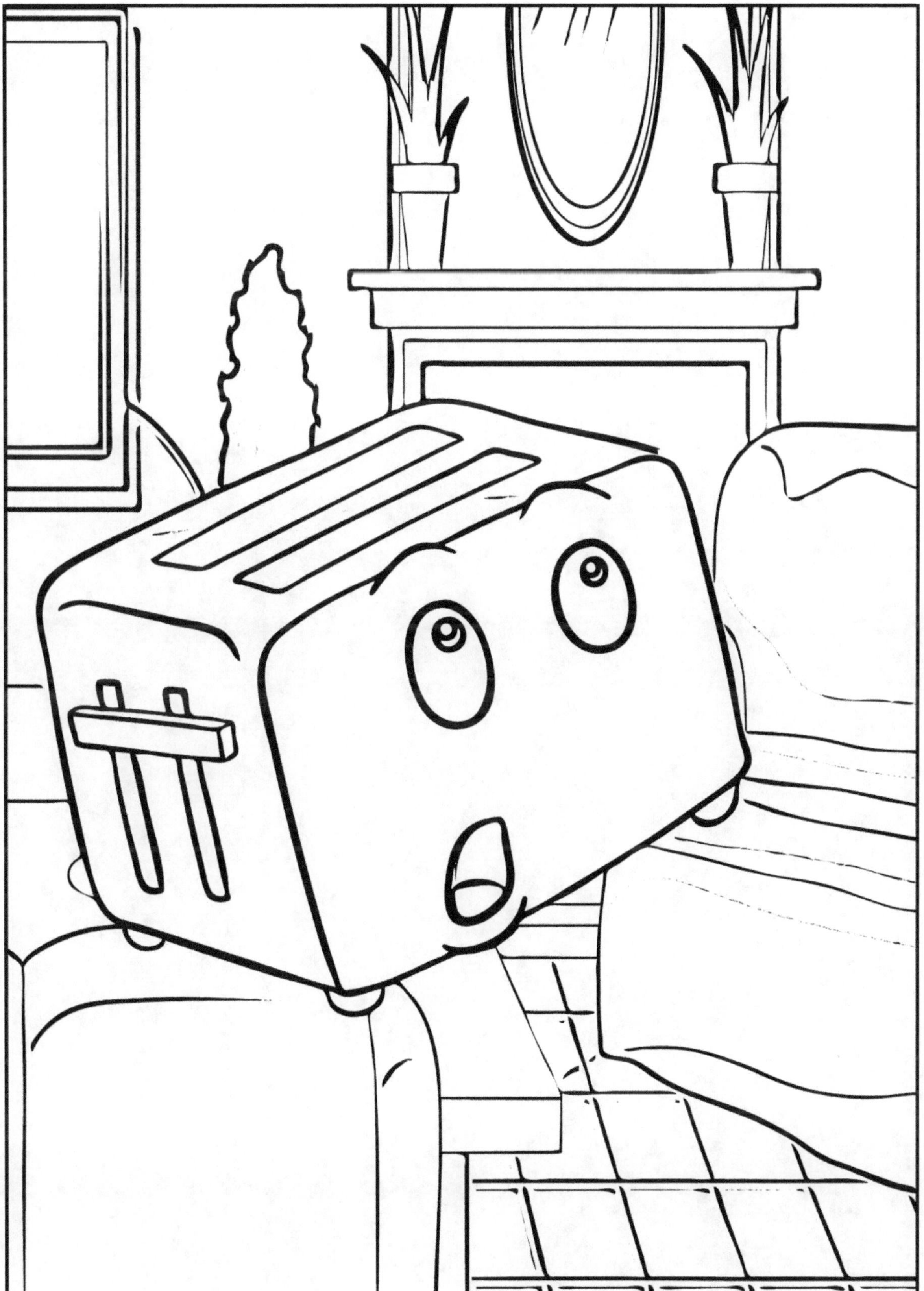

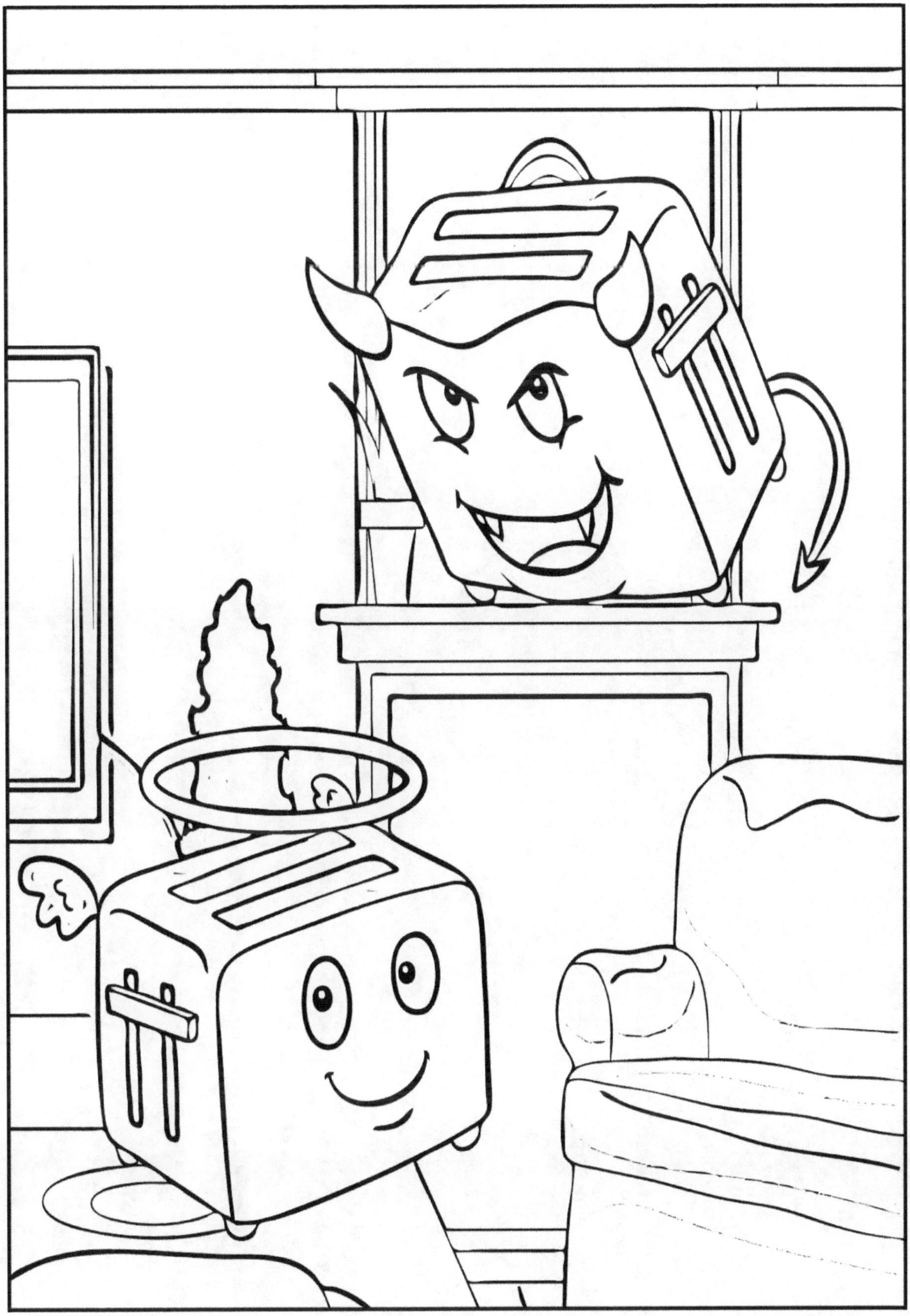

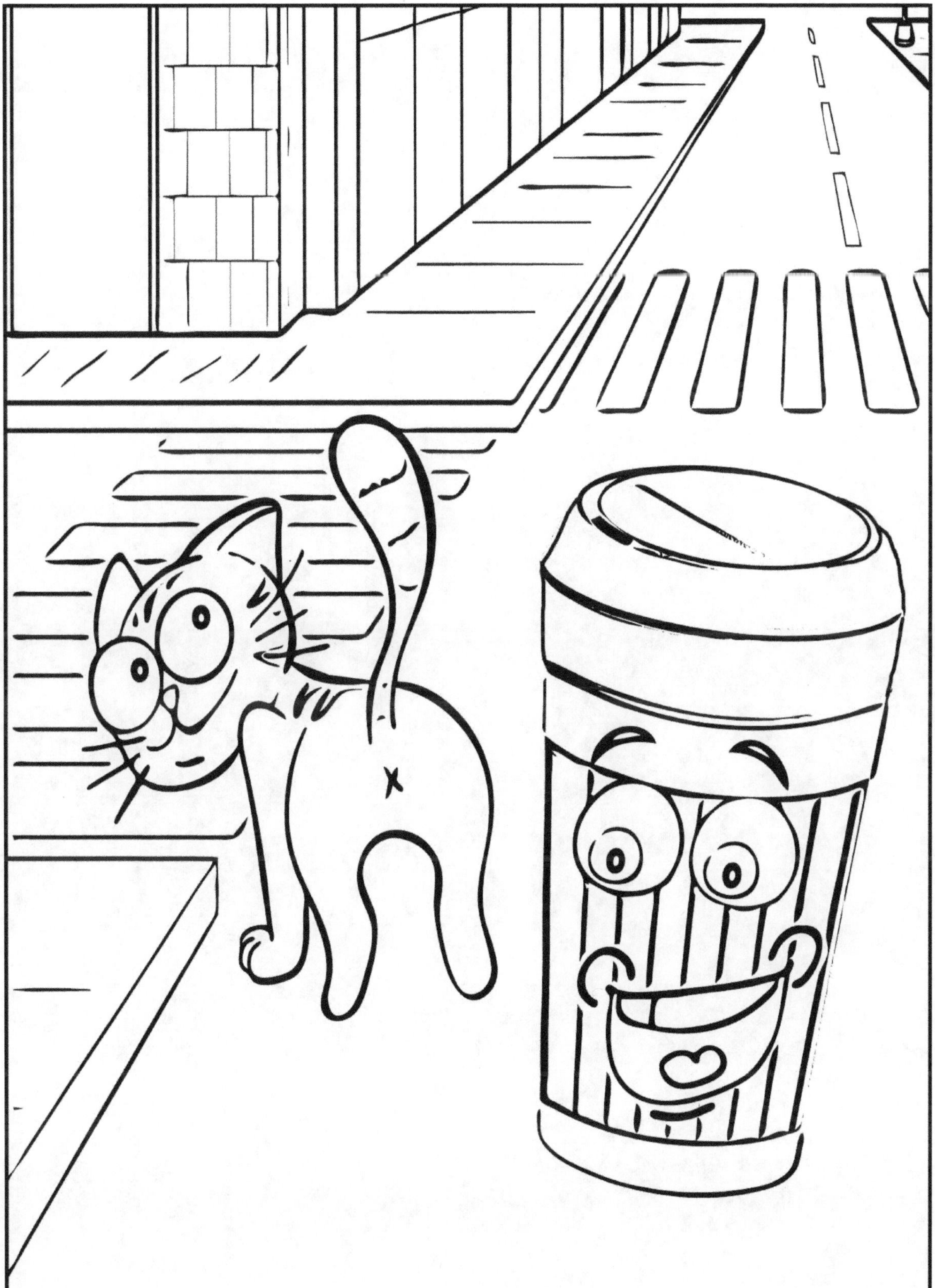

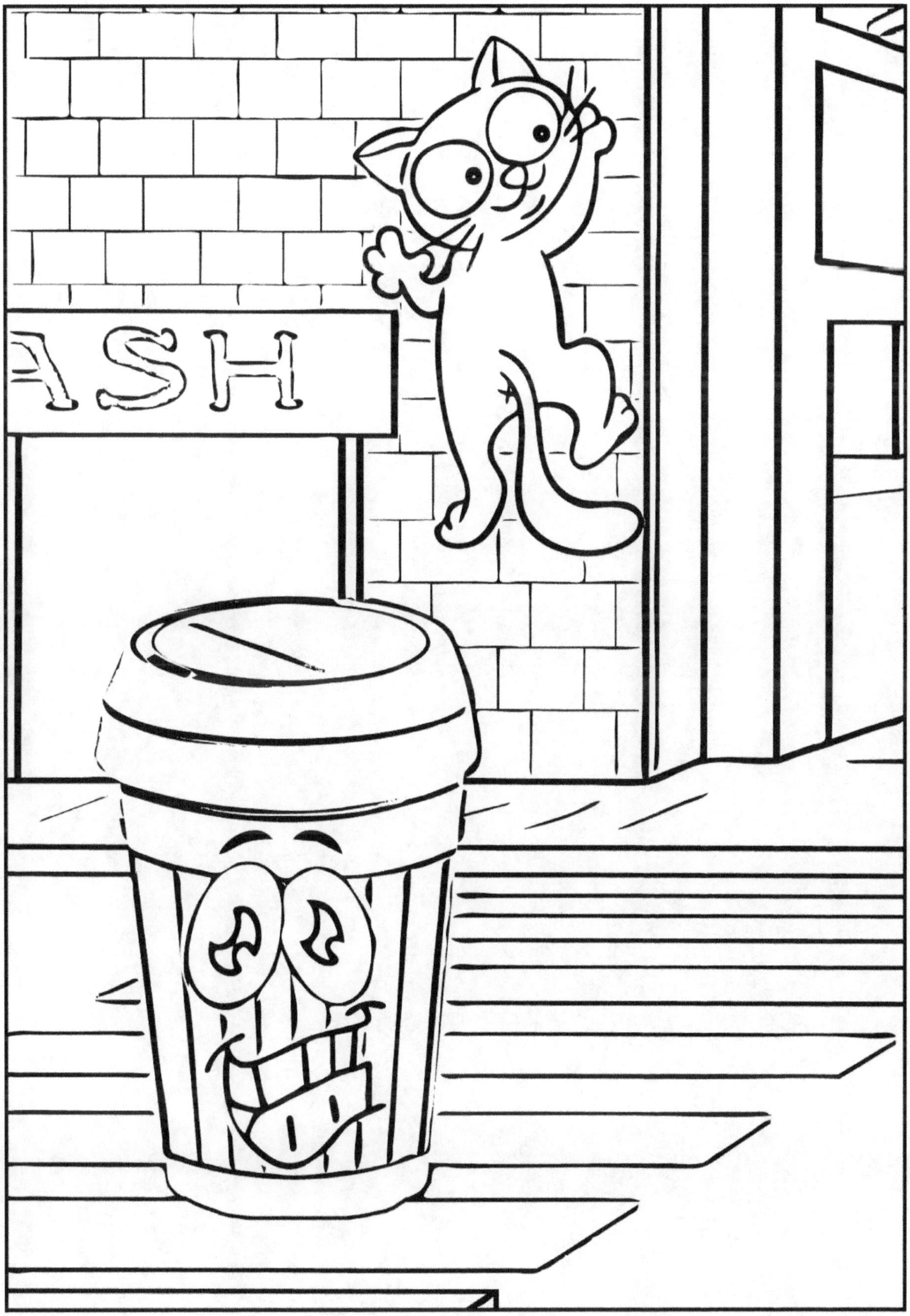
ASH

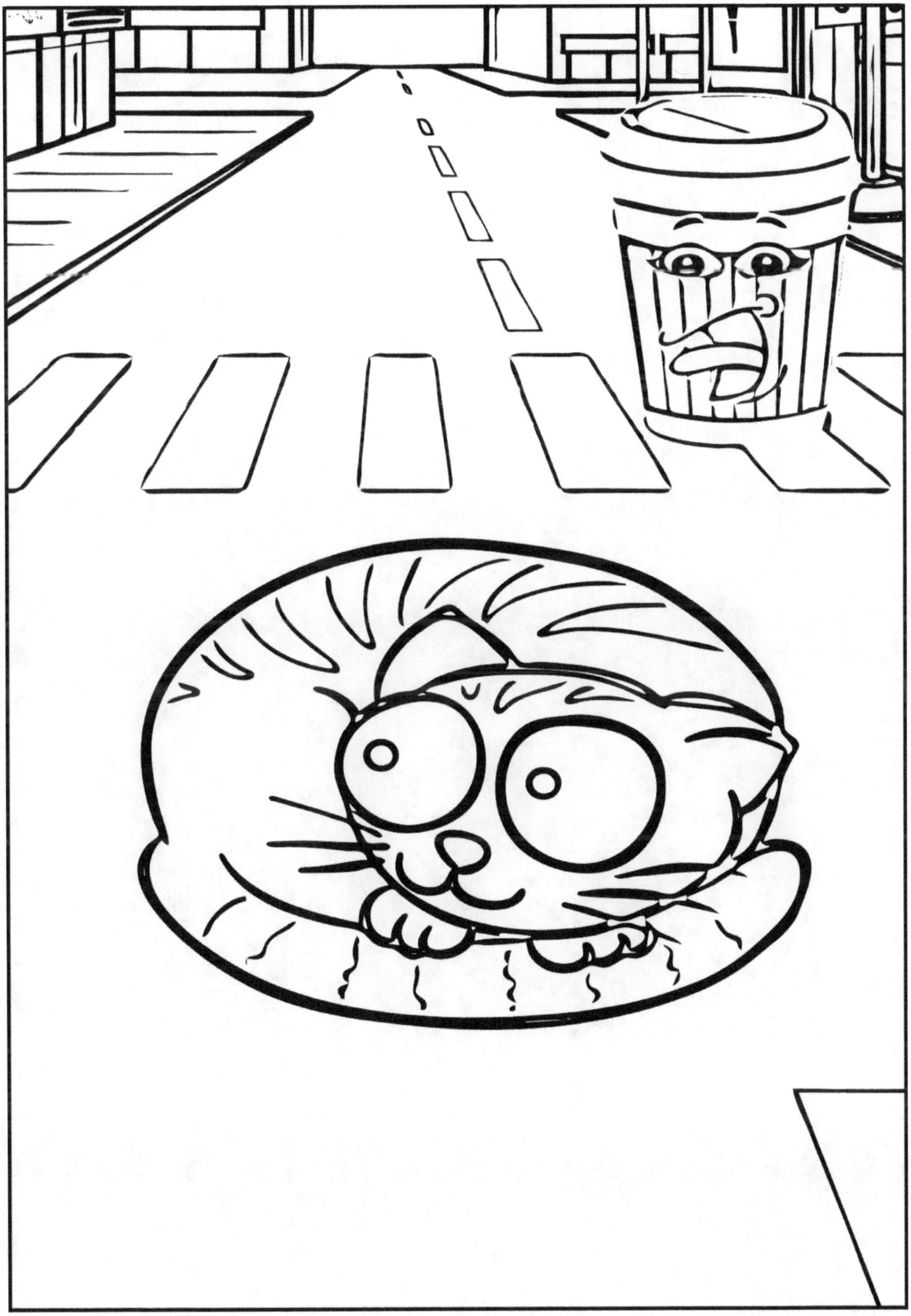

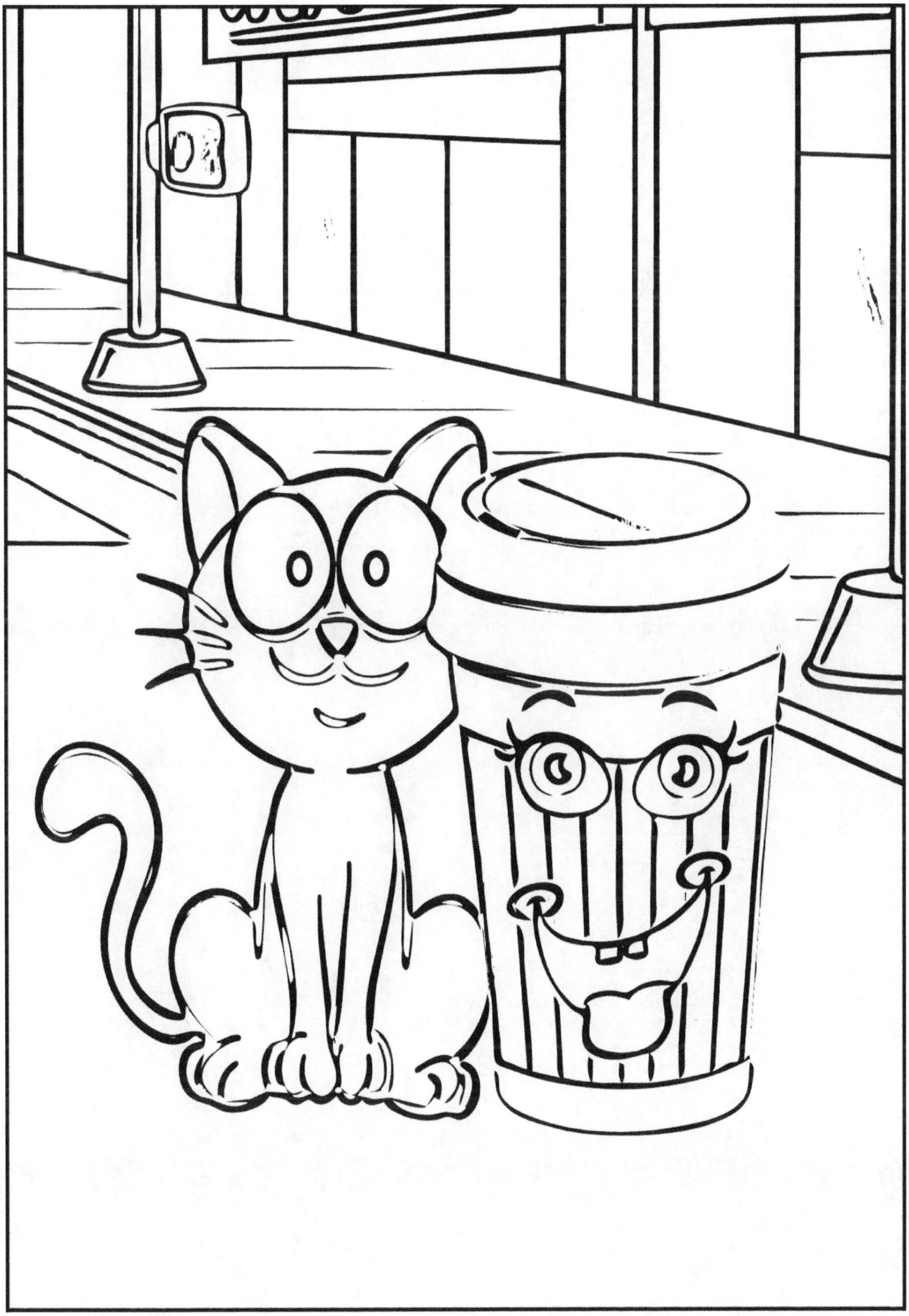

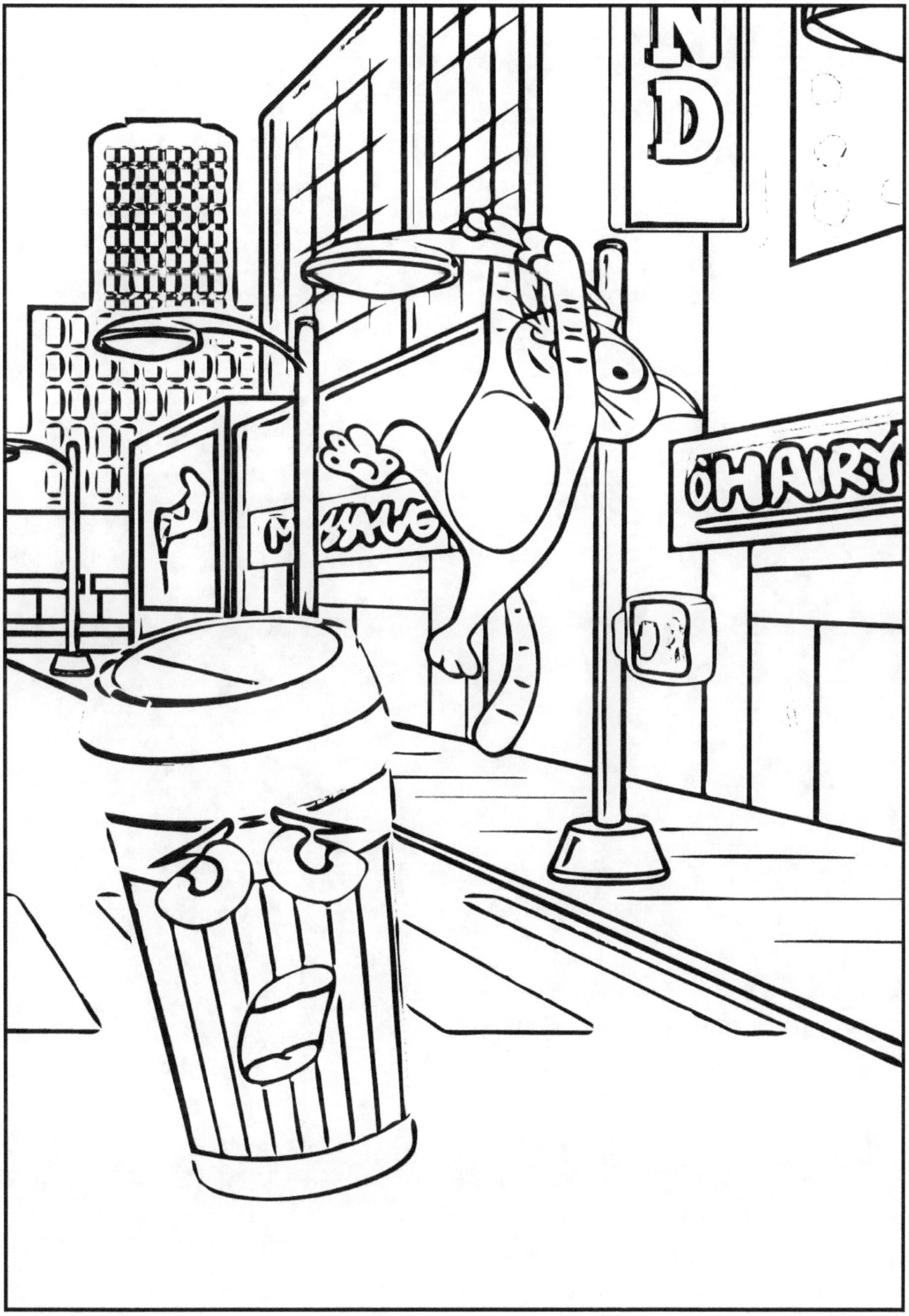
ND
ÖHAIRY

www.ingramcontent.com/pod-product-compliance
Lightning Source LLC
Chambersburg PA
CBHW080610180526
45168CB00007B/2854
9781517574208